HOW SMAR

TEST YOUR

MOVIE & TV

IQ

Pamela Horn

BLACK DOG & LEVENTHAL PUBLISHERS

NEW YORK

Published by

Black Dog & Leventhal Publishers Inc.
151 West 19th Street
New York, New York 10011

Distributed by

Workman Publishing Company
708 Broadway
New York, New York 10003

ISBN: 0-9637056-8-7

CONTENTS

Introduction

How smart are you? We can't answer that question for you generally, but this book certainly can determine your standing among the experts in movie and television knowledge — or at least with some of your family members and friends.

After taking the quizzes spanning Dabbler, Smarter-Than-Most, and Genius levels, calculating exactly what kind of masterful grasp of movies and TV you have will be the easy part.

Each level has an equal number of movie and television questions totaling two hundred questions in all. To get a true reading on your ability, take the tests adhering to the allotted time limits stated at the beginning of each section. The questions are all multiple choice. There are no tricks, but just compelling, fascinating, and strange entertainment trivia.

Once you complete a test, check the answer key at the end of that section and tally up your scores. Now you are equipped with all the information you need to spin the wheel and verify in seconds where your level of mastery lies.

All you have to do is turn to the front cover, and line up the number you answered correctly in the window on the scoring wheel. There are windows for each test level, so you can see how you fared with the Dabbler, Smarter-Than-Most, and Genius questions, as well as cumulatively.

DABBLER Movie Questions

Time limit: 30 minutes

1   **Who was the real man whose life was the subject of the movie *The Elephant Man*?**
    a. John Hurt
    b. David Merrick
    c. John Bartholemew
    d. P. T. Barnum
    e. John Merrick

2   **Who wrote and directed *Star Wars*?**
    a. Steven Spielberg
    b. Ron Howard
    c. Oliver Stone
    d. George Lucas
    e. Frances Ford Coppola

3   **In what movie did British actor Sydney Greenstreet make his film debut?**
    a. *Casablanca*
    b. *The Maltese Falcon*
    c. *Across the Pacific*
    d. *Between Two Worlds*
    e. *They Died With Their Boots On*

4   **The film *Saturday Night Fever* popularized which music and dance trend?**
    a. Country/Western
    b. Lambada
    c. Disco
    d. Rock and Roll
    e. New Wave

5 From what movie is this immortal line: "We made him an offer he couldn't refuse."?

   a. *Little Caesar*
   b. *Public Enemy*
   c. *The Godfather*
   d. *White Heat*
   e. *The Sting*

6 Who said: "Round up all the usual suspects"?

   a. Claude Rains in *Casablanca*
   b. Dan Ackroyd in *Dragnet*
   c. Kirk Douglas in *The Detective*
   d. George Raft in *Scarface*
   e. Trevor Howard in *The Third Man*

7 What is Cary Grant's real name?

   a. Bryant Fleming
   b. Stephen Richards
   c. Archibald Leach
   d. Mark Canfield
   e. Marion Michael Morrison

8 Who is Allen Stewart Konisberg?

   a. Stewart Granger
   b. Alan Alda
   c. Steve Allen
   d. Jimmy Stewart
   e. Woody Allen

9 Who played Jezebel in the movie *Jezebel?*

   a. Carole Lombard
   b. Bette Davis
   c. Olivia de Havilland
   d. Vivian Leigh
   e. Paulette Goddard

10 Who played in the 1929 screen version of *The Virginian*?

    a. Dustin Farnum
    b. Gary Cooper
    c. Owen Wister
    d. James Drury
    e. Joel McCrea

11 Who played Stanley Kowalski, Fletcher Christian, Emiliano Zapata and Marc Antony?

    a. Al Pacino
    b. Jack Lemmon
    c. Robert Duvall
    d. Marlon Brando
    e. James Mason

12 Who won the Oscar for best-supporting actor in the movie *City Slickers*?

    a. Jack Palance
    b. Robin Williams
    c. Daniel Stern
    d. Billy Crystal
    e. Bruno Kirby

13 Norman Bates is to Anthony Perkins as Hannibal Lecter is to:

    a. Bramwell Fletcher
    b. Tommy Lee Jones
    c. Whit Bissell
    d. Scott Glenn
    e. Anthony Hopkins

14 "Moon River" was the theme song for:

    a. *Women's World*
    b. *Roman Holiday*
    c. *Breakfast at Tiffany's*
    d. *September Affair*
    e. *Sabrina*

15 What film starring Cary Grant and Grace Kelly took place on the Cote d'Azur?

a. *Dial M For Murder*
b. *High Society*
c. *To Catch a Thief*
d. *Mogambo*
e. *The Swan*

16 Match the actor to the film in which he played a courtroom lawyer:

1. Spencer Tracy	a. *Compulsion*
2. Gregory Peck	b. *Judgement at Nuremberg*
3. Henry Fonda	c. *Inherit the Wind*
4. Richard Widmark	d. *To Kill a Mockingbird*
5. James Stewart	e. *Young Abe Lincoln*

17 Match the cast with the film in which they appeared:

1. Marilyn Monroe, Hugh Marlowe, Gregory Ratoff, George Sanders   a. *Juarez*

2. James Stewart, Ruth Hussey, Roland Young, Virginia Weidler   b. *All About Eve*

3. Bette Davis, Claude Rains, Walter Abel, Jerome Cowan   c. *Mrs. Skeffington*

4. Gladys Cooper, Nigel, Bruce, Reginald Denny, Joan Fontaine   d. *The Philadelphia Story*

5. Bette Davis, Claude Rains, Brian Aherne, John Garfield   e. *Rebecca*

18 What actor "came to dinner" in the movie co-starring Katharine Hepburn?

a. Cary Grant
b. John Barrymore
c. Sidney Poitier
d. James Baskett
e. Rossano Brazzi

19 What is the theme song of *Bonnie and Clyde*?

a. "Orange Blossom Special"
b. "Foggy Mountain Breakdown"
c. "Muleskinner Blues"
d. "Dueling Banjos"
e. "Wreck on the Highway"

20 Who played Michael Keaton's feline love-interest in *Batman Returns*?

a. Michelle Pfieffer
b. Kim Basinger
c. Sean Young
d. Eartha Kitt
e. Julie Newmar

21 Name the two warring gangs in *West Side Story*?

a. The Tigers and the Jets
b. The Sharks and the Hurricanes
c. The Cyclones and the Jets
d. The Jets and the Sharks
e. The Bloods and the Crips

22 Who played Holly Golightly's landlord in *Breakfast at Tiffany's*?

a. Moroni Olsen
b. Mickey Rooney
c. Frank Orth
d. Lee J. Cobb
e. Norman Fell

23 Match the casts with their films:

1. Elizabeth McGovern,   a. *The Color Purple*
   Meg Mundy, Donald
   Sutherland, M.
   Emmet Walsh   b. *Diner*
2. Keith Carradine,
   Christopher Guest,
   Stacy Keach, Randy
   Quaid
3. Timothy Daly, Ellen   c. *Mona Lisa*
   Barkin, Paul Reiser,
   SteveGuttenberg
4. Danny Glover,   d. *Ordinary People*
   Margaret Avery,
   Leonard Judison,
   Dana Ivey
5. Cathy Tyson, Sammi   e. *The Long Riders*
   Davis, Rod Bedall,
   Robbie Coltrane

24 What did Francis Ford Coppola win his first Oscar for?

a. *Patton*
b. *The Godfather*
c. *Finian's Rainbow*
d. *You're a Big Boy Now*
e. *The Conversation*

25 What movie won Frank Sinatra an Oscar and revived his career?

a. *On the Town*
b. *The Manchurian Candidate*
c. *From Here to Eternity*
d. *High Society*
e. *The Man with a Golden Arm*

26 For what movie did Cher win her Oscar for Best Actress?

a. *Come Back to the Five and Dime, Jimmy Dean, Jimmy Dean*

b. *The Witches of Eastwick*

c. *Moonstruck*

d. *Silkwood*

e. *Mask*

27 Match each science fiction thriller with its plot line:

1. *Gremlins*

a. A group of space explorers on a routine mission are tricked into bringing an extremely adaptable life form on board.

2. *Invasion of the Body Snatchers*

b. The crew travels back in time to retrieve two humpback whales in order to save the Earth from certain destruction.

3. *Alien*

c. An inventor obtains a cute, exotic pet for his son and is warned against three things. The rules are broken and the creature spawns hordes of vicious monsters.

4. *Star Trek IV - The Voyage Home*

d. The population of Santa Rosa, California, is replaced by a group of emotionless, soulless aliens.

5. *Blade Runner*

e. A bounty hunter is out to terminate four escaped androids who are thought to be dangerous.

28 What movie paired Marlon Brando with Eva Marie Saint?

a. *The Wild One*
b. *On the Waterfront*
c. *The Young Lions*
d. *The Chase*
e. *The Ugly American*

29 Match the Woody Allen characters with the film in which they appear:

1. Virgil Starkwell	a. *Love and Death*
2. Fielding Mellish	b. *Annie Hall*
3. Alvy Singer	c. *Take the Money and Run*
4. Boris Grushenko	d. *Sleeper*
5. Miles Monroe	e. *Bananas*

30 Who directed *The Sting*?

a. Brian De Palma
b. George Roy Hill
c. John Boorman
d. Hal Ashby
e. Robert Altman

31 Match the film with the role played by Groucho in the following Marx Brothers films:

1. *Horsefeathers*	a. Rufus T. Firefly
2. *A Night At the Opera*	b. Dr. Quackenbush
3. *A Day At the Races*	c. Professor Wagstaf
4. *Animal Crackers*	d. Otis B. Driftwood
5. *Duck Soup*	e. Captain Spalding

32 James Cagney won the Best Actor Oscar for:

a. *The Public Enemy*
b. *Mister Roberts*
c. *Man of a Thousand Faces*
d. *White Heat*
e. *Yankee Doodle Dandy*

33 In what movie did Marilyn Monroe, Betty Grable and Lauren Bacall move into an expensive high-rise and live above their means in order to meet a wealthy husband?

   a. *Women's World*
   b. *How to Marry a Millionaire*
   c. *The Group*
   d. *Sex and the Single Girl*
   e. *Gentlemen Prefer Blondes*

34 Match the John Wayne character with the movie:

   1. Nelson Brittles   a. *The Searchers*
   2. Ethan Edwards   b. *Stagecoach*
   3. John T. Chance   c. *She Wore a Yellow Ribbon*
   4. Rooster Cogburn   d. *Rio Bravo*
   5. The Ringo Kid   e. *True Grit*

DABBLER Movie Answers

(Score 1 point for each correct answer unless otherwise indicated.)

1. e
2. d
3. b   In 1941 Sydney Greenstreet made his film debut in the *Maltese Falcon* as a sinister rogue who coveted the gold falcon from Malta.
4. c   John Travolta starred in this film as Tony Manero, the gyrating disco king at "2001 Odyssey."
5. c   *The Godfather.* This line was spoken four times in the movie. It was said by Michael Corleone to Kay (Diane Keaton) about an offer Don Corleone made to the bandleader; by Vito to Johnny Fontaine about Woltz; by Sonny Corleone to Michael about the Tattaglias; and by Michael to Fredo about Moe Greene.
6. a   When Claude Rains gave this order it was referring to the German search in Casablanca for a spy.
7. c
8. e
9. b   Bette Davis received her second Academy Award for her role as *Jezebel* in 1938.

10. b   Gary Cooper. Dustin Farnum was in the 1914 version; Joel McCrea in 1945; and James Drury in the 1964 television series. Owen Wister wrote the novel.

11. d   Marlon Brando played Stanley Kowalski in *A Streetcar Named Desire*(1951); Fletcher Christian in *Mutiny on the Bounty*(1962); Emiliano Zapata in *Viva Zapata*(1952); and Marc Antony in *Julius Caesar*(1953).

12. a

13. e

14. c

15. c

16. 1 c, 2 d, 3 e, 4 b, 5 a (Score 1 point if all are correct, 1/2 if 3 are correct).

17. 1 b, 2 d, 3 c, 4 e, 5 a (Score 1 point if all are correct, 1/2 if 3 are correct).

18. c   Sidney Poitier, Katharine Hepburn, and Spencer Tracy starred in the movie *Guess Who's Coming to Dinner* (1967). Hepburn won an Academy Award for her performance.

19. b

20. a

21. d

22. b   Mickey Rooney's character's name was Mr. Yunioshi.

23. 1 d, 2 e, 3 b, 4 a, 5 c (Score 1 point if all are correct, 1/2 if 3 are correct).

24. a   *Patton*, Best Screenplay.

25. c.

26. c   Cher won the Academy Award in 1987 for her role in *Moonstruck* as Loretta Castorini.

27. 1 c, 2 d, 3 a, 4 b, 5 e (Score 1 point if all are correct, 1/2 if 3 are correct).

28. b

29. 1 d, 2 c, 3 a, 4 e, 5 b (Score 1 point if all are correct, 1/2 if 3 are correct).

30. b

31. 1 c, 2 a, 3 b, 4 e, 5 d (Score 1 point if all are correct, 1/2 if 3 are correct).

32. e

33. b

34. 1 c, 2 a, 3 d, 4 e, 5 b (Score 1 point if all are correct, 1/2 if 3 are correct).

DABBLER TV Questions

Time limit: 30 minutes

1 What character did Art Carney play in *The Honeymooners?*

   a. Tom Bradford
   b. Larry Melman
   c. Ed Norton
   d. Jimmy Olson
   e. Ralph Kramden

2 Who is famous for calling out, "Honey, I'm home!"?

   a. Ozzie Nelson
   b. Ricky Ricardo
   c. Ward Cleaver
   d. Dick Van Dyke
   e. Clarence Day, Sr.

3 What program is known for the line, "To boldly go where no man has gone before."?

   a. *Star Trek*
   b. *Bonanza*
   c. *The Twilight Zone*
   d. *The Big Valley*
   e. *Star Trek: The Next Generation*

4 In the television show *Hogan's Heroes*, who played Hogan?

   a. John Banner
   b. Robert Clary
   c. Bob Crane
   d. Richard Dawson
   e. Al Hodge

5 What is Mr. Rogers' first name?

a. Jim
b. Fred
c. Bill
d. John
e. Paul

6 In *The Brady Bunch*, what was the name of Alice's boyfriend the butcher?

a. Sol
b. Mel
c. Charlie
d. Sam
e. Ralph

7 Who was the voice of Charlie in the television show *Charlie's Angels*?

a. Lorne Greene
b. James Garner
c. Joseph Conrad
d. James Arness
e. John Forsythe

8 What show made the phrase "Book 'em, Danno" famous?

a. *Baretta*
b. *The Mod Squad*
c. *Streets of San Francisco*
d. *Hawaii Five-O*
e. *Mannix*

9 Laurie Partridge grew up to be a lawyer. What is this prosecutor's name?

a. Abigail Greene
b. Grace Van Owen
c. Julie March
d. Ann Kelsey
e. C. J. Lamb

10 Pair the crime fighting partners:

1. Scarecrow
2. Magruder
3. McMillan
4. Starsky
5. Cagney

a. Hutch
b. Mrs. King
c. Wife
d. Lacey
e. Loud

11 Match the characters with their co-workers:

1. Alice
2. Gopher
3. Mary
4. Hawkeye
5. Leland

a. Julie, Dr. Bricker, Isaac
b. Ted, Mr. Grant, Murray
c. Vera, Mel, Flo
d. Victor, Stewart, Roxanne
e. Margaret, Frank, Klinger

12 Match each character with his/her show:

1. Maurice, the warlock
2. Carlton, the doorman
3. Maynard G. Krebs
4. The Log Lady
5. Adam

a. *Northern Exposure*
b. *Dobie Gillis*
c. *Twin Peaks*
d. *Bewitched*
e. *Rhoda*

13 Match each school with the TV show in which it appears:

1. Whitman High
2. Fillmore High
3. Springfield Elementary
4. James Buchanan High
5. Madison High School

a. *The Simpsons*
b. *Room 222*
c. *Our Miss Brooks*
d. *The Brady Bunch*
e. *Welcome Back, Kotter*

14 What was the original name of *The Ed Sullivan Show?*

a. *The Late Show*
b. *Texaco Star Theater*
c. *Broadway Spotlight*
d. *Your Show of Shows*
e. *The Toast of the Town*

15 Who was the voice of Bugs Bunny?

    a. George Burns
    b. Mel Tillis
    c. Mel Blanc
    d. "Fritz" Freling
    e. Chuck Jones

16 Match each character with his or her TV boss:

1. Rob Petrie	a. Douglas Brachman
2. Hazel	b. Shirley Partridge
3. Stewart Markowitz	c. George Baxter
4. Hawkeye Pierce	d. Alan Brady
5. Reuben Kincaid	e. Colonel Blake

17 What are you watching if you choose this listing? Match the scene with the TV show:

1. George, Elaine, and Kramer meet for lunch at Monk's Cafe.	a. *A Different World*
2. Mary Jo loses Suzanne's pearls in a salad bar.	b. *Newhart*
3. Dick and Joanna can't get Stephanie to perform her chores.	c. *Cheers*
4. Cliff is convinced that his neighbor is Adolf Hitler.	d. *Designing Women*
5. Whitley and Jaleesa plan a surprise party for Dwayne.	e. *Murphy Brown*
6. Miles, Jim and Frank attend a men's weekend retreat.	f. *Seinfeld*

18 Which soap opera includes the following cast of characters? Clint, Marty, Andrew, Dorian, Rachel, Bo, and Luna

   a. *One Life To Live*
   b. *Loving*
   c. *Guiding Light*
   d. *Another World*
   e. *The Young and the Restless*

19 On what soap opera would you find the following places: The Goal Post, Pine ValleyUniversity, and Cortland Manor?

   a. *Search for Tomorrow*
   b. *Days of Our Lives*
   c. *All My Children*
   d. *General Hospital*
   e. *As The World Turns*

20 Match each cast with its sitcom:

   1. Conrad Bain, Esther Rolle, Bea Arthur, Rue McClanahan — a. *Filthy Rich*
   2. Tim Reid, Robert Harper, Tony Burton, Daphne Maxwell Reid — b. *Golden Girls*
   3. Dixie Carter, Conrad Bain, Dana Plato, Todd Bridges — c. *Maude*
   4. Dixie Carter, Delta Burke, Slim Pickens, Forrest Tucker — d. *Diff'rent Strokes*
   5. Bea Arthur, Estelle Getty, Betty White, Rue McClanahan — e. *Frank's Place*

21 Who played these *Saturday Night Live* characters?

   1. Linda Richmond — a. Dana Carvey
   2. Gumby — b. John Belushi
   3. Emily Litella — c. Gilda Radner
   4. Samurai Tailor — d. Mike Myers
   5. Garth Elgard — e. Eddie Murphy

22 Match the offspring with his or her parents:

1. Maggie	a. Phyllis and Lars Lindstrom
2. Mallory	b. Marge and Homer Simpson
3. Bess	c. Danny Williams
4. Lamont	d. Elyse and Steven Keaton

23 Match the host with his game show:

1. Monty Hall	a. *Tick-Tac-Dough*
2. Art Fleming	b. *Family Feud*
3. Richard Dawson	c. *Let's Make a Deal*
4. Peter Marshall	d. *The $25,000 Pyramid*
5. Dick Clark	e. *Jeopardy*

24 Which actor played the Lone Ranger on TV?

a. Guy Madison
b. George Hamilton
c. Clayton Moore
d. Dean Cain
e. George Reeves

25 Match the spin-off with the original television show:

1. *McHales's Navy*	a. *Fernwood 2-Night*
2. *Mary Hartman, Mary Hartman*	b. *Sanford Arms*
3. *Petticoat Junction*	c. *Broadside*
4. *Sanford and Son*	d. *Pete and Gladys*
5. *December Bride*	e. *Green Acres*

26 Chuckles the Clown died on a famous episode of what show?

a. *All in the Family*
b. *The Bob Newhart Show*
c. *The Dick Van Dyke Show*
d. *The Mary Tyler Moore Show*
e. *My Mother the Car*

27 What is the name of *Cheers* regular Norm's wife?

  a. Frances
  b. Maris
  c. Helen
  d. Gail
  e. Vera

28 Jethro and Elly May were the children on which show?

  a. *Green Acres*
  b. *Petticoat Junction*
  c. *The Big Valley*
  d. *The Beverly Hillbillies*
  e. *Mama's Family*

29 Identify the talk show host:

1. This host has admitted to being fired 36 times in 18 years.   a. Jack Paar
2. This host's show trademark featured a large mouth.   b. Sally Jesse Raphael
3. This *Tonight Show* regular guest later failed on a late night talk show on the Fox network.   c. Joey Bishop
4. Hugh Downs was this host's sidekick.   d. Joan Rivers
5. Regis Philbin was this host's sidekick.   e. Morton Downey, Jr.

30 What was the name of the boat that shipwrecked Gilligan, the Skipper, the Howells, Mary Ann, Ginger, and the Professor?

  a. Dolphin Daycruiser
  b. S. S. Guppie
  c. Hawaiian Cruiser
  d. S. S. Minnow
  e. The Skipjack

31 Identify the characters from Andy Griffith's town of Mayberry:

1. Bea	a. the town drunk
2. Otis	b. the druggist
3. Ellie	c. the deputy
4. Floyd	d. Andy's aunt
5. Barney	e. Mayberry's barber

32 Bob Eubanks hosted which show?

a. *The Dating Game*
b. *The Newlywed Game*
c. *Concentration*
d. *The Price is Right*
e. *The Gong Show*

33 Match the cast with their prime-time soap:

1. Mia Farrow, Ryan O'Neal, Lee Grant, Ruth Warrick	a. *Melrose Place*
2. Jane Wyman, Mel Ferrer, Lana Turner, Cesar Romero	b. *Knots Landing*
3. Heather Locklear, Rock Hudson, Diahann Carroll, Joan Collins	c . *Falcon Crest*
4. Heather Locklear, Andrew Shue, Courtney Thorn-Smith, Daphne Zuniga	d. *Peyton Place*
5. Ted Shackelford, Joan Van Ark, Michele Lee, William Devane	e. *Dynasty*

34 Match the celebrity spokesperson with the endorsed product:

1. Ricardo Montalban	a. *Pop Secret*
2. Janine Turner	b. *Weight Watchers*
3. Richard Petty	c. *Chevrolet*
4. Kathleen Sullivan	d. *STP*
5. Annie Potts	e. *Chrysler*

35 Match the fictional spokespersons with their products:

1. Rosie
2. Mr. Whipple
3. Madge
4. Mrs. Olsen
5. Speedy

a. *Folgers*
b. *Palmolive Dishwashing Liquid*
c. *Bounty*
d. *Alka Seltzer*
e. *Charmin'*

36 McLean Stevenson, best known for the hit series M*A*S*H, left the 4077th and went on to star in several major flops. Which of the following failed shows did he not headline?

a. *Hello Larry*
b. *In the Beginning*
c. *The Fanelli Boys*
d. *Condo*
e. *Celebrity Challenge of the Sexes*

DABBLER TV Answers

(Score 1 point for each correct answer unless otherwise indicated.)

1. c
2. b
3. a
4. c
5. b
6. d
7. e   After *Charlie's Angels*, John Forsythe went on to star in the long-running prime time soap opera *Dynasty*.
8. d
9. b
10. 1 b, 2 e, 3 c, 4 a, 5 d (Score 1 point if all correct, 1/2 point if 3 are correct).
11. 1 c, 2 a, 3 b, 4 e, 5 d (Score 1 point if all correct, 1/2 point if 3 are correct).
12. 1 d, 2 e, 3 b, 4 c, 5 a (Score 1 point if all correct, 1/2 point if 3 are correct).
13. 1 b, 2 d, 3 a, 4 e, 5 c (Score 1 point if all correct, 1/2 point if 3 are correct).

14. e
15. c
16. 1 d, 2 d, 3 a, 4 e, 5 b (Score 1 point if all correct, 1/2 point if 3 are correct).
17. 1 f, 2 d, 3 b, 4 c, 5 a, 6 e (Score 1 point if all correct, 1/2 point if 3 are correct).
18. a
19. c
20. 1 c, 2 e, 3 d, 4 a, 5 b (Score 1 point if all correct, 1/2 point if 3 are correct).
21. 1 d, 2 e, 3 c, 4 b, 5 a (Score 1 point if all correct, 1/2 point if 3 are correct).
22. 1 b, 2 d, 3 a, 4 e, 5 c (Score 1 point if all correct, 1/2 point if 3 are correct).
23. 1 c, 2 e, 3 b, 4 a, 5 d (Score 1 point if all correct, 1/2 point if 3 are correct).
24. c
25. 1 c, 2 a, 3 e, 4 b, 5 d (Score 1 point if all correct, 1/2 point if 3 are correct).
26. d
27. e
28. d

29. 1 b, 2 e, 3 d, 4 a, 5 c (Score 1 point if all correct, 1/2 point if 3 are correct).
30. d
31. 1 d, 2 a, 3 b, 4 e, 5 c (Score 1 point if all correct, 1/2 point if 3 are correct).
32. b   The *Newlywed Game* was a long-running game show featuring couples in their first year of marriage answering questions about their relationship.
33. 1 d, 2 c, 3 e, 4 a, 5 b (Score 1 point if all correct, 1/2 point if 3 are correct).
34. 1 e, 2 c, 3 d, 4 b, 5 a (Score 1 point if all correct, 1/2 point if 3 are correct).
35. 1 c, 2 e, 3 b, 4 a, 5 d (Score 1 point if all correct, 1/2 point if 3 are correct).
36. c

SMARTER-THAN-MOST
Movie Questions

Time limit: 30 minutes

1 Who directed the 1951 movie of Tennessee William's play *A Streetcar Named Desire*?

a. Fred Zinnemann
b. George Stevens
c. Joseph L. Mankiewicz
d. John Huston
e. Elia Kazan

2 Match the quote to the movie:

1. "I'm more or less particular about whom my wife marries."	a. *It Happened One Night*
2. "How did you get into that dress-with a spray gun?	b. *The Quiet Man*
3. "Kapplemeister, strike up the violas! My regiment leaves at dawn."	c. *His Girl Friday*
4. "I proved once and for all the limb is mightier than the thumb."	d. *Duck Soup*
5. "He'll regret it to his dying day, if he lives that long."	e. *Road to Rio*

3 Which actor appeared in *all* of these movies? *Lost Horizon, Mr. Smith Goes to Washington, Stagecoach, Gone with the Wind, Our Town, It's a Wonderful Life,* and *High Noon*

a. Guy Kibbee
b. Thomas Mitchell
c. Hume Cronyn
d. H. B. Warner
e. Ward Bond

4 *Beloved Infidel* **was based on author Sheilah Graham's affair with:**

a. F. Scott Fitzgerald
b. Ernest Hemingway
c. David O. Selznick
d. Jean-Paul Sartre
e. Wendell Wilkie

5 Match the director with his gangster film:

1. Michael Curtiz
2. William Wellman
3. Mervyn Le Roy
4. Raoul Walsh
5. Howard Hawks

a. *Little Caesar*
b. *White Heat*
c. *Scarface*
d. *Angels with Dirty Faces*
e. *The Public Enemy*

6 Match the couple with the actors who portrayed them:

1. Alex Forrest & Dan Gallagher
2. Linda & David Howard
3. Audrey Hankel & Charles Driggs
4. Beth & Calvin Jarret
5. Lucy Honeychurch & George Emerson

a. Mary Tyler Moore & Donald Sutherland
b. Helena Bonham Carter & Julian Sands
c. Melanie Griffith & Jeff Daniels
d. Glenn Close & Michael Douglas
e. Julie Hagerty & Albert Brooks

7 Who were the women in Clare Boothe Luce's *The Women?*

a. June Allyson, Barbara Stanwyck, Shelley Winters, and Nina Foch
b. Norma Shearer, Rosalind Russell, Paulette Goddard, and Joan Crawford
c. Rosalind Russell, Joan Crawford, June Allyson, and Barbara Stanwyck
d. Joan Fontaine, Rosalind Russell, Paulette Goddard, June Allyson
e. Ann Miller, Ann Sheridan, Joan Blondell, June Allyson

8 "I believe in America. America has made my fortune..." is the opening line from:

a. *A Place in the Sun*
b. *Pride of the Yankees*
c. *The Great Gatsby*
d. *Meet John Doe*
e. *The Godfather*

9 Who directed *Bonnie and Clyde?*

a. Sam Peckinpah
b. Arthur Hiller
c. Bob Rafelson
d. William Friedkin
e. Arthur Penn

10 Which Clint Eastwood film featured the following cast: George Kennedy, Jack Cassidy, Thayer David and Vonette McGee?

a. *The Outlaw Josey Wales*
b. *The Eiger Sanction*
c. *Magnum Force*
d. *High Plains Drifter*
e. *Heartbreak Ridge*

11 Match the director with his/her film:

1. Sidney Poitier   a. *The Hitch-Hiker*
2. Jose Ferrer   b. *Buck and the Preacher*
3. Paul Newman   c. *The Great Man*
4. Ida Lupino   d. *Easy Rider*
5. Dennis Hopper   e. *Rachel, Rachel*

12 Which film does not belong?

a. *The Little Shop of Horrors*
b. *The King of Marvin Gardens*
c. *Chinatown*
d. *The Hustler*
e. *Hell's Angels on Wheels*

13 In which film did **Al Pacino** have his first major movie role?

a. *The Panic in Needle Park*
b. *Scarecrow*
c. *Dog Day Afternoon*
d. *Serpico*
e. *Me, Natalie*

14 What short story was *Apocalypse Now* based on?

a. "Heart of Darkness"
b. "The Island of Dr. Moreau"
c. "The Killer "
d. "Night Bus "
e. "The Secret Sharer"

15 In what movie does the character **Archibald Leach** appear?

a. *Notorious*
b. *A Fish Called Wanda*
c. *Father Goose*
d. *Young Frankenstein*
e. *None But the Brave*

16 Match the cast with its film:

1. Matthew Broderick, Cary Elwes, Denzel Washington, Jihmi Kennedy	a. *The Heartbreak Kid*
2. Cybill Shepherd, Charles Grodin, Jeannie Berlin, Eddie Albert	b. *Platoon*
3. Forest Whitaker, Tom Berenger, Johnny Depp, Willem Dafoe	c. *A New Leaf*
4. Walter Matthau, James Coco, Elaine May, Jack Weston	d. *The Outsiders*
5. Diane Lane, Tom Waits, Matt Dillon, Rob Lowe	e. *Glory*

17 In what film's opening sequence does the narrator say, "The poor dope — he always wanted a pool."

a. *Father of the Bride*
b. *The Asphalt Jungle*
c. *Sunset Boulevard*
d. *A Place in the Sun*
e. *Mr. Blandings Builds His Dream Home*

18 Match the film character with her appropriate description:

1. Joan Crawford as Mildred Pierce

a. An ambitious young actress insinuates herself into the good graces of a top Broadway star, then tries to destroy her.

2. Lana Turner as Georgia

b. A factory worker's affair results in her pregnancy and eventually her murder.

3. Anne Baxter as Eve

c. A prim English missionary in an African village learns about survival and sensuality on the eve of World War I.

4. Katharine Hepburn as Rose Sayers

d. A mother works as a waitress to give her daughter everything, then takes the rap for a murder she didn't commit.

5. Shelley Winters as Alice Tripp

e. An alcoholic is seduced, built into a superstar, and then destroyed.

19 What do John Barrymore, Frederic March, and Spencer Tracy have in common?

a. They all had affairs with Katharine Hepburn.
b. They were all Catholics.
c. They all played *Dr. Jekyll and Mr. Hyde.*
d. They all won two Academy Awards.
e. They were all MGM contract actors for most of their careers.

20 Match the film couples with the actors who portrayed them:

1. Ellie Andrews & Peter Warne
2. Emily Webb & George Gibb
3. Lola Frohlich & Immanuel Rath
4. Vickie Lester & Norman Maine
5. Don Birnam and Helen St. James

a. Janet Gaynor & Fredric March, *A Star is Born*
b. Claudette Colbert & Clark Gable, *It Happened One Night*
c. Martha Scott & WilliamHolden, *Our Town*
d. Marlene Dietrich & Emil Jannings, *The Blue Angel*
e. Jane Wyman & Ray Milland, *The Lost Weekend*

21 What film, based on a novel by Thomas Dixon, had its black characters portrayed by white actors in blackface?

a. *Green Pastures*
b. *The Emperor Jones*
c. *The Birth of a Nation*
d. *Darktown Jubilee*
e. *Intolerance*

22 Match the actors and films with their famous lines:

1. Cary Grant in *Arsenic & Old Lace*
2. Elizabeth Taylor in *Who's Afraid of Virginia Woolf?*
3. Jimmy Cagney in *White Heat*
4. Greta Garbo in *Camille*
5. Gloria Swanson in *Sunset Boulevard*

a. "Made it Ma. Top of the world!"
b. "I always look well when I'm near death."
c. "I am big. It's the pictures that got small."
d. "Insanity runs in my family. It practically gallops."
e. "I swear, if you existed, I'd divorce you."

23 Match the screen couples with the actors who portrayed them:

1. Aurora Greenway & Garrett Breedlove
2. Tess McGill & Jack Trainer
3. Mookie & Tina
4. Anne & John Millaney
5. Halley Reed & Cliff Stern

a. Andie MacDowell & Peter Gallagher
b. Mia Farrow & Woody Allen
c. Shirley MacLaine & Jack Nicholson
d. Melanie Griffith & Harrison Ford
e. Rosie Perez & Spike Lee

24 In *sex, lies and videotape*, who played Graham Dalton, the man who seduced women into revealing their sexual desires and frustrations on tape?

a. Rob Lowe
b. Matt Dillon
c. Alec Baldwin
d. Kevin Bacon
e. James Spader

25 Match the actors with the action-heroes they portrayed:

1. Mel Gibson	a. Mick Dundee in *'Crocodile' Dundee*
2. Michael Douglas	b. Max Rodeatansky in *The Road Warrior*
3. Harrison Ford	c. Indiana Jones in *Raiders of the Lost Ark*
4. Paul Hogan	d. Jack Colton in *Romancing the Stone*
5. Arnold Schwarzenegger	e. Jack Slater in *Last Action Hero*

26 What film featured characters named Ted Spindler, Richard Adams, Jack Godell, and Kimberly Wells?

    a. *Chinatown*
    b. *The Towering Infemo*
    c. *The China Syndrome*
    d. *Coming Home*
    e. *Comes a Horseman*

27 Which film does not belong?

    a. *Looking for Mr. Goodbar*
    b. *Days of Heaven*
    c. *Places in the Heart*
    d. *American Gigolo*
    e. *The Cotton Club*

28 For what movie did John Huston win Oscars for Best Direction and Screenplay, and his father, Walter Huston, win an Oscar for Best Supporting Actor?

    a. *The Treasure of the Sierra Madre*
    b. *The Maltese Falcon*
    c. *In This Our Life*
    d. *The African Queen*
    e. *Duel in the Sun*

29 Who directed the film *My Brilliant Career?*

a. Gillian Armstrong
b. Alison Anders
c. Lee Grant
d. Jane Campion
e. Lina Wertmuller

30 Match the leading man who played opposite Doris Day in the following films:

1. David Niven	a. *Calamity Jane*
2. Richard Widmark	b. *Please Don't Eat the Daisies*
3. Rock Hudson	c. *Pajama Game*
4. Howard Keel	d. *Pillow Talk*
5. John Raitt	e. *The Tunnel of Love*

31 Which film marked Angelica Huston's film debut?

a. *The Postman Always Rings Twice*
b. *This is Spinal Tap*
c. *The Last Tycoon*
d. *Prizzi's Honor*
e. *Sinful Davey*

32 Garbo talks! What were her first on screen words?

a. "I suppose I'm just drifting."
b. "Want to kiss me, ducky?"
c. "Gimme a viskey. Ginger ale on the side. And don' be stingy, ba-bee"
d. "I want to be alone."
e. "You mustn't kid Mother, dear. I was a married woman before you were bom."

SMARTER-THAN-MOST
Movie Answers

1. a
2. 1 c; 2 e; 3 d; 4 a; 5 b (Score 1 point if all correct, 1/2 point if 3 are correct).
3. b   Thomas Mitchell was an actor of great versatility whose characters ranged from comic to tragic, and humane to evil.
4. a
5. 1 d; 2 e; 3 a; 4 b; 5 c   Real life menace in the twenties in America provided the new gangster theme for film. (Score 1 point if all correct, 1/2 point if 3 are correct).
6. 1. d *Fatal Attraction*
   2. e *Lost in America*
   3. c *Something Wild*
   4. a *Ordinary People*
   5. b *A Room With A View*
   (Score 1 point if all correct, 1/2 point if 3 are correct).
7. b
8. e   This line was spoken by the undertaker, Bonasera.
9. e
10. b
11. 1 b; 2 c; 3 e; 4 a; 5 d (Score 1 point if all correct, 1/2 point if 3 are correct).
12. d   *The Hustler*. Jack Nicholson appeared in all the movies except *The Hustler*.
13. e   *Me, Natalie* in 1968.
14. a   "Heart of Darkness."
15. b   John Cleese played Archibald Leach.
16. 1 e; 2 a; 3 b; 4 c.; 5 d. (Score 1 point if all correct, 1/2 point if 3 are correct).
17. c   *Sunset Boulevard* (1950) was directed by Billy Wilder, who also co-wrote the script with Charles Brackett and D. M. Marsham Jr. William Holden plays Gloria Swanson's "kept man" who encourages her false hopes as a fading star. Holden is the "poor dope" referred to in the opening scene.
18. 1 d *My Son John*
    2 e *The Bad and the Beautiful*
    3 a *All About Eve*
    4 c *African Queen*
    5 b *A Place in the Sun*
    (Score 1 point if all correct, 1/2 point if 3 are correct).

19. c

20. 1 b; 2 c; 3 d; 4 a; 5 e (Score 1 point if all correct, 1/2 point if 3 are correct).

21. c   *Birth of a Nation* in 1914. In the same year *Darktown Jubilee* was the first film with an all black cast.

22. 1. d; 2. e; 3. a; 4. b; 5. c (Score 1 point if all correct, 1/2 point if 3 are correct).

23. 1 c   *Terms of Endearment*
    2 d   *Working Girls*
    3 e   *Do the Right Thing*
    4 a   *sex, lies and videotape*
    5 b   *Crimes and Misdemeanors*
       (Score 1 point if all correct, 1/2 point if 3 are correct).

24. e

25. 1. b; 2. d; 3. c; 4. a; 5. e (Score 1 point if all correct, 1/2 point if 3 are correct).

26. c   *The China Syndrone*. The actors portraying each character were as follows:
         Ted Spindler — Wilford Brimley
         Richard Adams — Michael Douglas
         Jack Godell — Jack Lemmon
         Kimberly Wells — Jane Fonda

27. c   *Places in the Heart* starred John Malkovich. The others featured Richard Gere.

28. a

29. a

30. 1. b; 2. e; 3. d; 4. a; 5. c (Score 1 point if all correct, 1/2 point if 3 are correct)

31. e   *Sinful Davey* (1969)

32. c   This famous line is from the film *Anna Christie*.

SMARTER-THAN-MOST
TV Questions

Time limit: 30 minutes

1 How did Walter Cronkite end his nightly news broadcasts?

   a. "And so it goes."
   b. "And that's the way it is."
   c. "That's the news for now."
   d. "Signing off until tomorrow."
   e. "Good night and good news."

2 What actress played Frasier Crane's first wife on *Cheers*?

   a. Bebe Neuwirth
   b. Shelley Long
   c. Emma Thompson
   d. Meryl Streep
   e. Carrie Fisher

3 "Great Caesar's Ghost" was whose favorite expletive?

   a. Captain Gregg in *The Ghost and Mrs. Muir*
   b. The Chief in *Get Smart*
   c. Perry White in *Superman*
   d. Colonel Potter in *M*A*S*H*
   e. Martin Crane in *Frasier*

4 In *I Dream of Jeannie*, who was the attending psychiatrist at NASA who would observe the strange arrangement between astronaut Tony and his "Jeannie"?

   a. Dr. Pierce
   b. Dr. Bellows
   c. Dr. Bricker
   d. Dr. Smith
   e. Dr. Spock

5 Who was the star of the soap opera spoof *Mary Hartman, Mary Hartman*?

a. Renee Taylor
b. Ellen Burstyn
c. Louise Lasser
d. Shelley Fabares
e. Janet Margolin

6 Who were the daughters in the Robinson family of the 1960s show *Lost in Space*?

a. Penny and June
b. Lucy and June
c. Penny and Cindy
d. Ellie and Judy
e. Judy and Penny

7 Which show did not feature Jayne Meadows?

a. *I've Got a Secret*
b. *Medical Center*
c. *The Honeymooners*
d. *It's Not Easy*
e. *The Art Linkletter Show*

8 Match the main character to the TV Western:

1. *The Big Valley*   a. Jody O'Connell
2. *Branded*   b. Jim Hardie
3. *Have Gun Will Travel*   c. Jarrod Barkley
4. *Buckskin*   d. Jason McCord
5. *Tales of Wells Fargo*   e. Paladin

9 Do you know the married names for these TV characters?

1. Carol Kester   a. Gerard
2. Rhoda Morgenstern   b. Baxter
3. Kate Miller   c. Penobscot
4. Georgette Franklin   d. Bondurant
5. Margaret Houlihan   e. Douglas

10 Which *Thirtysomething* stars are married in real life?

a. Michael and Nancy
b. Gary and Hope
c. Gary and Ellen
d. Elliot and Melissa
e. Elliot and Nancy

11 Nancy Walker played Rhoda's mother. What was her name?

a. Sally
b. Bea
c. Ida
d. Doris
e. Sadie

12 On *The Beverly Hillbillies*, who was Miss Hathaway's boss?

a. Mr. Baxter
b. Mr. Dithers
c. Mr. Mooney
d. Mr. Carlson
e. Mr. Drysdale

13 Match the television family with their television show:

1. The Lawrences
2. The Davises
3. The Ingalls
4. The Nashes
5. The Monroes

a. *My World and Welcome to It*
b. *Little House on the Prairie*
c. *Family*
d. *Family Affair*
e. *Please Don't Eat the Daisies*

14 These TV shows have "shows within shows." Make the correct matches:

1. *Home Improvement*
2. *Murphy Brown*
3. *The Dick Van Dyke Show*
4. *Mary Tyler Moore*
5. *The Simpsons*

a. "The Alan Brady Show"
b. "The Happy Homemaker"
c. "The Itchy & Scratchy Show"
d. "F.Y.I"
e. "Tool Time"

15 Who is the odd one out?

a. Joe Gannon
b. Jason Seaver
c. Hamilton Burger
d. Lilith Sternin-Crane
e. Leonard McCoy

16 Match the couples:

1. Barney Fife
2. David Addison
3. Gomer Pyle
4. Fred Munster
5. Matt Dillon

a. Miss Kitty
b. Lou Ann Povey
c. Maddie Hayes
d. Thelma Lou
e. Lily

17 Match the plot sketch with the show:

1. Crockett and Tubbs declare war on drug dealers.
2. Former boxer takes job as live-in housekeeper
3. Tim fends off Lorelei's suspicions about Martin O'Hara's behavior.
4. Coach Reeves argues with the principal about the basketball budget.
5. Kevin Arnold sends a love note to Winnie.

a. *The White Shadow*
b. *My Favorite Martian*
c. *Miami Vice*
d. *The Wonder Years*
e. *Who's the Boss?*

18 Who was not a Huxtable child?

    a. Denise
    b. Sandra
    c. Vanessa
    d. Rudy
    e. Claire

19 Match the actress with her crime fighting show:

1. Peggy Lipton	a. *Honey West*
2. Teresa Graves	b. *The Mod Squad*
3. Helen Hayes	c. *The Avengers*
4. Anne Francis	d. *The Snoop Sisters*
5. Diana Rigg	e. *Get Christie Love*

20 Which science fiction show features this cast of characters: Jake, Kira, Dax, O'Brien, and Dr. Bashir?

    a. *Moonbase Alpha*
    b. *Star Trek: Deep Space Nine*
    c. *Buck Rogers in the 25th Century*
    d. *Babylon Five*
    e. *Battlestar Galactica*

21 Match the hosts with their programs:

1. Edward R. Murrow	a. *You Are There*
2. Alistair Cooke	b. *Omnibus*
3. Lowell Thomas	c. *See It Now*
4. Walter Cronkite	d. *Meet the Press*
5. Lawrence Spivak	e. *High Adventure*

22 Match the sergeants with their television shows:

1. Sgt. Yemana	a. *Hill Street Blues*
2. Sgt. Garcia	b. *Barney Miller*
3. Sgt. "Pepper" Anderson	c. *CHiPS*
4. Sgt. Esterhaus	d. *Zorro*
5. Sgt. Gatraer	e. *Police Woman*

23 Aside from being children's favorite neighbor, Mr. Rogers is also:

a. a licensed school teacher
b. a licensed medical doctor
c. an ordained Presbyterian minister
d. an accomplished banjo player
e. all of the above

24 What television personality failed his first audition as a radio broadcaster and, discouraged, took a job at a bank?

a. Geraldo Rivera
b. Phil Donahue
c. Bob Costas
d. Regis Philbin
e. Greg Kinnear

25 Which successful television producer and personality receives only $300 a week in pocket money from his accountant?

a. Bill Cosby
b. Dick Clark
c. Merv Griffin
d. Johnny Carson
e. Tom Arnold

26 Who played Clarabelle the Clown on *The Howdy Doody Show* and was fired because of a dispute with management?

a. Soupy Sales
b. Fred Rogers
c. Casey Kasem
d. Jerry Lewis
e. Bob Keeshan

27 Match the doctor with his or her show:

1. Dr. Sam Beckett
2. Dr. Monica Quartermaine
3. Dr. Dick Richard
4. Dr. Stephen Kiley
5. Dr. Alex Stone

a. *China Beach*
b. *Quantum Leap*
c. *Marcus Welby, M.D.*
d. *The Donna Reed Show*
e. *General Hospital*

28 What TV family lived at 704 Hauser Street?

a. The Cleavers
b. The Mitchells
c. The Cunninghams
d. The Jeffersons
e. The Bunkers

29 What do Jane Pauley and David Letterman have in common?

a. They both started their careers as weather forecasters.
b. They were in the same class at Ohio State.
c. Their first anchoring experience was when they co-anchored a local news broadcast.
d. They both come from Indiana.
e. All of the above

30 Selina Kyle was the real name of this character on *Batman*:

a. Catwoman
b. Bat Girl
c. Ilona, The Joker's helper
d. Wild Rosie
e. Mrs. Frost

31 Who were the Petries' neighbors on *The Dick Van Dyke Show*?

a. Alan and Sally Brady
b. Jack and Mary Fletcher
c. Jerry and Millie Helper
d. Joe and Julie Warner
e. Buddy and Pickles Sorrell

32 Who was not a writer of Sid Caesar's *Your Show of Shows?*

a. Sid Caesar
b. Mel Brooks
c. Steve Allen
d. Neil Simon
e. Carl Reiner

33 Of the following Laugh-In regulars, who remained with the show from its beginning to end?

a. Ruth Buzzi
b. Alan Sues
c. Judy Carne
d. Arte Johnson
e. JoAnne Worley

SMARTER-THAN-MOST
TV Answers

1. b
2. c   Emma Thompson. Bebe Neuwirth was Frasier's second wife, Lilith.
3. c
4. b
5. c
6. e
7. c
8. 1. c; 2. d; 3. e; 4. a; 5. b (Score 1 point if all are correct; 1/2 point if 3 are correct).
9. 1. d; 2. a; 3. e; 4. b; 5. c (Score 1 point if all are correct; 1/2 point if 3 are correct).
10. a
11. c
12. e

13. 1. c; 2. d; 3. b; 4. e; 5. a (Score 1 point if all are correct; 1/2 point if 3 are correct).
14. 1. e; 2. d; 3. a; 4. b; 5. c (Score 1 point if all are correct; 1/2 point if 3 are correct).
15. c. Hamilton Burger is the only attorney; the rest are doctors. Dr. Joe Gannon was on *Medical Center*; Dr. Jason Seaver was on *Growing Pains*; Dr. Lilith Sternin-Crane was on *Cheers*; Dr. Leonard McCoy was on *Star Trek*; Hamilton Burger was a district attorney on *Perry Mason*.
16. 1. d; 2. c; 3. b; 4. e; 5. a (Score 1 point if all are correct; 1/2 point if 3 are correct).

17. 1. c; 2. e; 3. b; 4. a; 5. d (Score 1 point if all are correct; 1/2 point if 3 are correct).
18. e
19. 1. b; 2. e; 3. d; 4. e; 5. a (Score 1 point if all are correct; 1/2 point if 3 are correct).
20. b
21. 1. c; 2. b; 3. e; 4. a; 5. e (Score 1 point if all are correct; 1/2 point if 3 are correct).
22. 1. b; 2. d; 3. e; 4. a; 5. e (Score 1 point if all are correct; 1/2 point if 3 are correct).
23. c
24. b
25. c Although Merv Griffin is now worth hundreds of millions of dollars, he needs to be put on this modest budget.
26. e
27. 1. b; 2. e; 3. a; 4. c; 5. d (Score 1 point if all are correct; 1/2 point if 3 are correct).
28. e On *All in the Family*, the Bunkers lived at this address in Queens, New York.
29. d
30. a
31. c
32. c

GENIUS Movie Questions

Time limit: 30 minutes

1 Who is Dith Pran?

a. A Korean man who befriends the members of the *M*A*S*H* unit
b. A character in Oliver Stone's movie about Vietnam, *Platoon*
c. One of Kurtz's followers in *Apocalypse Now*
d. A Cambodian photographer featured in *The Killing Fields*
e. A character in Lewis Milestone's Korean War classic *Pork Chop Hill*

2 Match the actress' real name with her stage name:

1. Margarita Carmin Cansino	a. Lee Grant
2. Camille Javal	b. Veronica Lake
3. Constance Ockleman	c. Rita Hayworth
4. Lyova Rosenthal	d. Theda Bara
5. Theodosia Goodman	e. Brigitte Bardot

3 Which one of the following was not their last film?

a. William Holden, *S.O.B.*
b. Carole Lombard, *To Be or Not To Be*
c. James Dean, *Rebel Without A Cause*
d. Peter Finch, *Network*
e. Jean Harlow, *Saratoga*

4 The film *Devotion* chronicled the life of what family?

a. The Curies
b. The Days
c. The Ekdahls
d. The Bröntes
e. The Barrymores

5 **What do the following actors have in common: Dinah Shore, Laurence Harvey, Robin Williams, Michael Landon, Theda Bara and John Garfield?**

    a. They all were/are devoted Christian Scientists.
    b. They all dropped out of high school and never went back.
    c. They each were married at least three times.
    d. They all were/are Jewish.
    e. They were all adopted.

6 Match the novel with the film it was made into:

1. *The House of Dr. Edwardes*, by Francis Beeding	a. *Julia*
2. *Some Must Watch*, by Ethel Lina White	b. *The Long Hot Summer*
3. *The Hamlet*, by William Faulkner	c. *The Spiral Staircase*
4. *Pentimento*, by Lillian Hellman	d. *Stage Fright*
5. *Man Running*, by Selwyn Jepson	e. *Spellbound*

7 Which film does not belong?

    a. *The Little Foxes*
    b. *The Man Who Came to Dinner*
    c. *Whatever Happened to Baby Jane*
    d. *All This and Heaven Too*
    e. *Now Voyager*

8 Match each "love" affair film with its leading woman:

1. *Love Me Tonight*	a. Irene Dunne
2. *Love Letters*	b. Audrey Hepburn
3. *Love Affair*	c. Jeanette MacDonald
4. *Love Happy*	d. Jennifer Jones
5. *Love in the Afternoon*	e. Marilyn Monroe

9 Match the actor or entertainer with the person who portrayed her on film:

1. Ruth Etting
2. Carole Lombard
3. Lillian Roth
4. Helen Morgan
5. Jeanne Eagels

a. Ann Blyth
b. Doris Day
c. Jill Clayburgh
d. Diana Ross
e. Kim Novak

10 Which does not belong?

a. *All About Eve*
b. *The Lost Weekend*
c. *A Letter to Three Wives*
d. *The Barefoot Contessa*
e. *Suddenly Last Summer*

11 What do Phyllis Calvert, Joanne Woodward, and Eleanor Parker have in common?

a. They all played opposite Paul Newman.
b. They all played opposite Joseph Cotten.
c. They all spent time in a psychiatric facility.
d. They all played women with split personalities.
e. They all were directed by King Vidor.

12 Match the cast with the film it appeared in.

1. Susannah York, Joan Greenwood, Albert Finney, Hugh Griffith
2. Clifton Webb, Lauren Bacall, Cornel Wilde, Fred MacMurray
3. Rhys Williams, Joan Crawford, Sterling Hayden, Ernest Borgnine
4. Sterling Hayden, James Whitmore, Marilyn Monroe, Sam Jaffe
5. Henry Fonda, Margaret Sullivan, Walter Brennan, Beulah Bondi

a. *Johnny Guitar*
b. *The Moon's Our Home*
c. *Tom Jones*
d. *Woman's World*
e. *Asphalt Jungle*

13 What do these actors have in common?
-**Katharine Hepburn** in *The Philadelphia Story*
-**Robert Montgomery** in *June Bride*
-**Jean Arthur** in *Mr. Smith Goes to Washington*
-**Alan Bates** in *A Kind of Loving*

a. They were all divorced.
b. They all quit the movie in the middle of filming and later returned to finish.
c. They were all drunk in a scene (or scenes).
d. They all were left at the altar.
e. They all received Oscar nominations.

14 Which film does not belong?

a. *Lenny*
b. *Valley of the Dolls*
c. *The French Connection*
d. *Peyton Place*
e. *A Hatful of Rain*

15 Match the actor with the writer he portrayed:

1. Gregory Peck   a. Oscar Wilde
2. Richard Chamberlain   b. Lord Byron
3. Peter Finch   c. Gustave Flaubert
4. Fredric March   d. F. Scott Fitzgerald
5. James Mason   e. Mark Twain

16 For which film did Robert Altman win the Best Direction Academy Award?

a. *The Player*
b. *M*A*S*H*
c. *Nashville*
d. *Short Cuts*
e. None of the above

17 Match each actor with his big screen debut:

1. Dustin Hoffman   a. *Taxi Driver*
2. Harvey Keitel   b. *The Tiger Makes Out*
3. Albert Brooks   c. *Tim*
4. Mel Gibson   d. *Valley of the Dolls*
5. Richard Dreyfuss   e. *Who's That Knocking at My Door?*

18 Match each actress with her big screen debut:

1. Natalie Wood
2. Meg Ryan
3. Melanie Griffith
4. Julia Roberts
5. Susan Sarandon

a. *Baja Oklahoma*
b. *Smile*
c. *Joe*
d. *Tomorrow is Forever*
e. *Rich and Famous*

19 Match the director with his or her film:

1. Diane Kurys
2. Wim Wenders

3. Pedro Almodovar
4. Stephen Frears
5. Agnieszka Holland

a. *My Beautiful Laundrette*
b. *What Have I Done to Deserve This?*
c. *Europa, Europa*
d. *Entre Nous*
e. *Alice in the Cities*

20 Elvis Lives! Match each story line with the corresponding Presley film:

1. Small-town boy becomes overnight sensation when signed by lady press agent to sing with her ex-husband's country band

a. *Double Trouble*

2. Young busboy on verge of delinquency gets his break when he s forced to sing at a New Orleans nightclub

b. *Girl Happy*

3. To pay for the motor he needs to race, Elvis has to win a hotel employees' talent contest

c. *Viva Las Vegas*

4. Elvis is a nightclub entertainer who finds love in Ft. Lauderdale during spring break

d. *Loving You*

5. A rock and roll singer finds love with an English heiress

e. *King Creole*

21 In *Last Tango in Paris*, Marlon Brando plays an American who despairs over the recent suicide of his wife. What is his wife's name?

    a. Jeanne
    b. Catherine
    c. Rosa
    d. Britches
    e. Eleanor

22 Match the director with her film:

1. Penelope Spheeris	a. *Fast Times at Ridgemont High*
2. Amy Heckerling	b. *Sticky Fingers*
3. Nancy Savoca	c. *True Love*
4. Caitlin Adams	d. *Pet Sematary*
5. Mary Lambert	e. *Wayne's World*

23 Match the following Ingmar Bergman films with their descriptions:

1. *Wild Strawberries*	a. A bedroom farce later adapted as Sondheim's *A Little Night Music*
2. *The Seventh Seal*	b. An old doctor reminisces and faces his life and his disappointments.
3. *The Virgin Spring*	c. A rape murder is avenged.
4. *Smiles of a Summer Night*	d. The story of a dying woman, her sisters and maid
5. *Cries and Whispers*	e. A knight challenges death to a game of chess to settle his fate.

24 Match the movie with the actress "that" starred in them:

1. *That Kind of Woman*	a. Shirley Temple
2. *That Certain Feeling*	b. Olivia de Havilland
3. *That Uncertain Feeling*	c. Sophia Loren
4. *That Hagen Girl*	d. Eva Marie Saint
5. *That Lady*	e. Merle Oberon

25 Who did not star in a Hitchcock film?

a. Karen Black
b. Joan Fontaine
c. Carole Lombard
d. Shirley MacLaine
e. Joan Bennett

26 Which actress, voted by *The Harvard Lampoon* as the "Worst Actress of the Year" later went on to win two Oscars?

a. Katharine Hepburn
b. Meryl Streep
c. Elizabeth Taylor
d. Jodie Foster
e. Jane Fonda

27 What do Mae West, Sophia Loren, and Jane Russell have in common?

a. They each married more than three times.
b. They all had breast reductions.
c. They all wrote autobiographies.
d. They all spent time in jail.
e. They all admitted having affairs with Marlene Dietrich.

28 Match the actor with the job he/she held before becoming famous:

1. Warren Beatty
2. Carol Burnett
3. Sean Connery
4. Yul Brynner
5. Maureen Stapleton

a. A trapeze artist
b. An artist's nude model
c. A construction worker on the Lincoln Tunnel
d. A coffin polisher
e. An usher in a movie theatre

29 Match the women with the films they directed:

1. Diane Keaton
2. Lina Wertmuller
3. Doris Doerrie
4. Zelda Baron
5. Kathryn Bigelow

a. *Men*
b. *Blue Steel*
c. *Heaven*
d. *Swept Away*
e. *Shag*

30 Match the cast with the film in which it appeared:

1. Helena Bonham Carter, Prunella Scales, James Wilby, Emma Thompson	a. *Enchanted April*
2. Joan Plowright, Polly Walker, Miranda Richardson, Alfred Molina	b. *Where Angels Fear to Tread*
3. Helena Bonham Carter, Daniel Day-Lewis, Rosemary Leach, Rupert Graves	c. *A Room with a View*
4. Helena Bonham Carter, Rupert Graves, Judy Davis, Giovanni Guidelli	d. *Howard's End*
5. Julie Christie, Sashi Kapoor, Greta Scaachi, Christopher Cazanove	e. *Heat and Dust*

31 What two-time Academy Award-winning actor started his acting career as a robot in the Theatre Guild's production of *R.U.R*?

a. Joseph Cotten
b. Burt Lancaster
c. Paul Newman
d. Kirk Douglas
e. Spencer Tracy

32 What do all these women have in common: Emily Clark, Harriet Brown, Jane Emerson, Gussie Berger, and Mary Holmquist?

a. They all auditioned for Melanie *Gone With the Wind*.
b. These were all names used by Greta Garbo when travelling 'incognito'.
c. They all were names used by Frances Gumm before she settled on Judy Garland.
d. They worked for Joan Crawford as nannies and were fired.
e. They were all famous stunt doubles.

33 Who are the only two women to be nominated for an Oscar for Best Direction?

a. Jane Campion for *The Piano*
b. Barbra Striesand for *Prince of Tides*
c. Penny Marshall for *Awakenings*
d. Lina Wertmuller for *Seven Beauties*
e. Lee Grant for *Tell Me a Riddle*

Genius Movie Answers

1. d   *The Killing Fields* chronicled his heroic struggle to escape the turmoil of the Pol Pot regime in Cambodia.
2. 1 c; 2 e; 3 b; 4 a; 5 d (Score 1 point if all are correct; score 1/2 point if 3 are correct).
3. c   James Dean filmed *Rebel Without a Cause* in 1955. He died in 1955, but *Giant*, his last film was released in 1956.
4. d
5. d
6. 1 e; 2 c; 3 b; 4 a; 5 d (Score 1 point if all are correct; 1/2 point if 3 are correct).
7. c   These are all Bette Davis films from the 1940's except for *Whatever Happened to Baby Jane?*, which was released in 1962.
8. 1 c; 2 d; 3 a; 4 e; 5 b (Score 1 point if all are correct; 1/2 point if 3 are correct).
9. 1 b; 2 c; 3 d; 4 a; 5 e (Score 1 point if all are correct; 1/2 point if 3 are correct).
10. b   All the other films were directed by Joseph L. Mankiewicz. *The Lost Weekend* was directed by Billy Wilder.
11. d   They all played women with split personalities: *Madonna of the Seven Moons*; *The Three Faces of Eve*; and *Lizzie* respectively.
12. 1 c; 2 d; 3 a; 4 e; 5 b (Score 1 point if all are correct; 1/2 point if 3 are correct).
13. c
14. d   The plots of the other four films revolve around drug addiction.

15. 1 d; 2 b; 3 a; 4 e; 5 c (Score 1 point if all are correct; 1/2 point if 3 are correct).
16. None of the above. Altman has never won an Oscar for directing.
17. 1 b; 2 e; 3 a; 4 c; 5 d (Score 1 point if all are correct; 1/2 point if 3 are correct).
18. 1 d; 2 e; 3 b; 4 a; 5 c (Score 1 point if all are correct; 1/2 point if 3 are correct).
19. 1 d; 2 e; 3 b; 4 a; 5 c (Score 1 point if all are correct; 1/2 point if 3 are correct).
20. 1 d; 2 e; 3 c; 4 b; 5 a (Score 1 point if all are correct; 1/2 point if 3 are correct).
21. c
22. 1 e; 2 a; 3 c; 4 b; 5 d (Score 1 point if all are correct; 1/2 point if 3 are correct).
23.
24. 1 c; 2 d; 3 e; 4 a; 5 b (Score 1 point if all are correct; 1/2 point if 3 are correct).
25. e
26. e
27. d   Mae West spent eight days in a New York City prison after her play *Sex* was closed by a police raid because of complaints from the Society for the Suppression of Vice. Sophia Loren spent seventeen days in Guididiario Prison for tax evasion. Jane Russell spent ninety-six hours in jail for reckless driving.
28. 1 c; 2 e; 3 d; 4 a; 5 b (Score 1 point if all are correct; 1/2 point if 3 are correct).
29. 1 c; 2 d; 3. a; 4 e; 5 b (Score 1 point if all are correct; 1/2 point if 3 are correct).
30. 1 d; 2 a; 3 c; 4 b; 5 e (Score 1 point if all are correct; 1/2 point if 3 are correct).
31. e
32. b
33. a and d (Score one point each)

GENIUS TV Questions

Time limit: 30 minutes

1 On the *Flintstones*, Fred and Barney belong to this lodge.

   a. The Keepers of the Brontosaurus
   b. The Loyal Order of Water Buffaloes
   c. The Loyal Clan of Bedrock
   d. The Rotary Club
   e. The Moose Lodge

2 Who played the police chief in the television show *The Mod Squad?*

   a. Adam Greer
   b. Broderick Crawford
   c. David Birney
   d. Robert Taylor
   e. Walter Abel

3 Match these successful television producers and writers with their hit shows:

   1. Marcy Carsey   a. *Designing Women*
   2. Linda Bloodworth-   b. *Soap*
      Thomason
   3. Susan Harris   c. *Murphy Brown*
   4. Diane English   d. *Roseanne*
   5. Debbie Allen   e. *A Different World*

4 What is the profession of Bob and Emily Hartley's ever-present neighbor, Howard, on the *Bob Newhart Show?*

   a. a dentist
   b. an insurance salesman
   c. a cruise boat captain
   d. an airline navigator
   e. a pilot

5 What was the name of *My Little Margie's* next door neighbor?

    a. Mr. Wilson
    b. Mrs. Odetts
    c. Mrs. Petrie
    d. Mr. Rogers
    e. Mrs. Winger

6 The cabbies on *Taxi* worked for which cab company?

    a. Blue Sky Cab Company
    b. City Cab Company
    c. Chelsea Cab Company
    d. Sunshine Cab Company
    e. Dover Cab Company

7 Match the cast with the show it appeared on:

1. Richard Crenna, Kathy Nolan, Michael Winkelman, Walter Brennan	a. *Petticoat Junction*
2. Bernadette Withers, Noreen Corcoran, John Forsythe, Jimmy Boyd	b. *Mr. Peepers*
3. Tony Randall, Wally Cox, Jack Warden, Marion Lorne	c. *The Real McCoys*
4. Edgar Buchanan, Bea Benaderet, Gunilla Hutton, Meredith MacRae	d. *To Rome with Love*
5. Walter Brennan, Joyce Menges, John Forsythe, Kay Medford	e. *Bachelor Father*

8 Match each dog with his television show:

1. Duke	a. *Dennis the Menace*
2. Buck	b. *The Brady Bunch*
3. Tiger	c. *My Three Sons*
4. Fremont	d. *The Beverly Hillbillies*
5. Tramp	e. *Married withChildren*

9 Where do these characters live on their TV shows?

1. Dwayne Schneider, *One Day at a Time*	a. Boulder
2. Edith Bunker, *All in the Family*	b. Brooklyn
3. Trixie Norton, *The Honeymooners*	c. Seattle
4. Mindy McConnell, *Mork and Mindy*	d. Indianapolis
5. Niles Crane, *Frasier*	e. Queens

10 What do Andy Griffith, James Stewart, Audie Murphy, and John Gavin all have in common?

a. They all played robbers in early television shows.
b. They were never married in any of their role.
c. They all played Destry in *Destry Rides Again*.
d. They never rode a horse in any of their television roles.
e. They all did their own stunts.

11 Match the actors with the soap opera role they appeared in before achieving stardom:

1. Demi Moore	a. Sara, *Search for Tomorrow*
2. Kevin Kline	b. Nola Aldrich, *The Doctors*
3. Morgan Freeman	c. Roy Bingham, *Another World*
4. Susan Sarandon	d. Woody Reed, *Search for Tomorrow*
5. Kathleen Turner	e. Jackie Templeton, *General Hospital*

12 What television actor and director thought he had "ears like Dumbo" and so had them surgically pinned back?

 a. Ron Howard
 b. Andy Griffith
 c. Don Knotts
 d. Michael Landon
 e. Ted Knight

13 What was the most money you could win on *What's My Line?*

 a. $30
 b. $50
 c. $75
 d. $100
 e. $500

14 Match the television personalities with their previously held jobs:

1. Larry King	a. Sold meat from a meat-packing plant in Kansas
2. Don Johnson	b. Bookkeeper
3. John Larroquette	c. Janitor at a Miami radio station
4. Bob Newhart	d. Disc Jockey
5. David Letterman	e. Weatherman

15 What precinct did Barney Miller work out of?

 a. 10th Precinct
 b. 11th Precinct
 c. 12th Precinct
 d. 13th Precinct
 e. 24th Precinct

16 Who was the voice of Jane Jetson?

 a. Shirley Jones
 b. Patricia Harty
 c. Penny Singleton
 d. June Lockhart
 e. Pamela Britton

17 CBS took this show off the air in 1969 because of censorship disputes. What show was this?

  a. *Omnibus*
  b. *The Smothers Brothers*
  c. *60 Minutes*
  d. *As the World Turns*
  e. *Laugh-in*

18 Which cook does not belong?

  a. Julia Child
  b. James Beard
  c. Pierre Franey
  d. Jeff Smith
  e. Martin Yan

19 Who were George and Gracie's next door neighbors?

  a. Molly and Jake Goldberg
  b. Patricia Marshall and her son Paul
  c. Mickey and Nora Grady
  d. George and Barbara Apple
  e. Blanche and Harry Morton

20 Who was the first host of *The Today Show*?

  a. Jack Paar
  b. John Cameron Swayze
  c. Steve Allen
  d. Ernie Kovacs
  e. Dave Garroway

21 What show are you watching?

1. Kookie loses Bailey's and Spencer's cars
2. Thirty-year-old paper boy lives with his parents
3. Chris builds an elaborate sculpture
4. Number 6 battles to preserve his individuality
5. Duncan 'Dunky' moves in with his aunt and uncle

a. *Northern Exposure*
b. *Dobie Gillis*
c. *The Prisoner*
d. *77 Sunset Strip*
e. *Get a Life*

22 Who killed Laura Palmer?

a. Leo
b. Bob
c. Leland
d. Bobby
e. The one-armed man

23 What was bailiff "Bull" Shannon's real first name?

a. Tiberius
b. Nostrodamus
c. Charles
d. Thor
e. Leslie

24 Which bizarre incident did not occur on *Mary Hartman, Mary Hartman*?

a. Neighbor drowns in chicken soup.
b. Child evangelist is electrocuted when his television falls into the bathtub.
c. Grandpa Shumway is arrested for exposing himself.
d. Wife beater impales himself on an aluminum Christmas tree.
e. Housewife campaigns to have her Aunt Dora made a saint because of her "remarkable raisin bread."

25 Who was Mrs. Calabash?

a. Jimmy Durante's nickname for his late wife
b. The head mistress of the orphanage where Jimmy Durante grew up
c. The owner of a Chicago rooming house where Durante and his wife had lived briefly after their marriage
d. Jimmy Durante's Sunday school teacher
e. The woman who gave Jimmy Durante voice lessons

26 *American Bandstand* was originally broadcast from:

a. Atlantic City, NJ
b. Providence, RI
c. Philadelphia, PA
d. Cleveland, OH
e. Baltimore, MD

27 Match the show with its location:

1. *The High Chaparral*   a. North Fork, New Mexico
2. *Have Gun, Will Travel* b. The Sierra Nevada
3. *Bonanza*   c. Arizona Territory
4. *The Rifleman*   d. Sweetwater, Arizona
5. *Bret Maverick*   e. San Francisco

28 Match the celebrity with the soap opera on which he/she guest starred:

1. Elizabeth Taylor   a. *Dynasty*
2. Donald Trump   b. *Santa Barbara*
3. Sammy Davis, Jr.   c. *General Hospital*
4. Henry Kissinger   d. *One Life to Live*
5. Dame Judith Anderson   e. *All My Children*

29 Who appeared on *Laugh In*, saying "Sock it to me"?

a. Gerald Ford
b. Jimmy Carter
c. Henry Kissinger
d. Chief Justice Earl Warren
e. Richard Nixon

30 What kind of car did Buz Murdock drive on *Route 66*?

a. a Thunderbird
b. a Corvette
c. a Mustang
d. a Ford Fairlane
e. a Chevrolet Impala

31 Who shot J.R.?

a. Lucy Ewing Cooper
b. Cliff Barnes
c. Sue Ellen Ewing
d. Kristin Shepard
e. Katherine Wentworth

32 Match the year with the television event:

1. 1971	a. Walter Cronkite passes the torch to Dan Rather
2. 1969	b. First broadcast of *Nightline*
3. 1970	c. *All in the Family* debuts
4. 1981	d. Viewers see men on the moon
5. 1980	e. The last year cigarette ads were seen

GENIUS TV Answers

1. b
2. a
3. 1 d; 2 a; 3 b; 4 c; 5 e (Score 1 point if all are correct; 1/2 point if 3 are correct).
4. d Howard doesn't actually fly the airplane; he is the navigator.
5. b
6. d
7. 1 c; 2 e; 3 b; 4 a; 5 d (Score 1 point if all are correct; 1/2 point if 3 are correct).
8. 1 d; 2 e; 3 b; 4 a; 5 c (Score 1 point if all are correct; 1/2 point if 3 are correct).
9. 1 d; 2 e; 3 b; 4 a; 5 c (Score 1 point if all are correct; 1/2 point if 3 are correct).
10. c
11. 1 e; 2 d; 3 c; 4 a; 5 c (Score 1 point if all are correct; 1/2 point if 3 are correct).
12. d
13. b
14. 1 c; 2 a; 3 d; 4 b; 5 e (Score 1 point if all are correct; 1/2 point if 3 are correct).
15. c
16. c
17. b
18. b James Beard is the only cook that did not have a television cooking series.
19. e
20. e
21. 1 d; 2 e; 3 a; 4 c; 5 b (Score 1 point if all are correct; 1/2 point if 3 are correct).
22. b & c Leland was possessed by Bob.
23. b
24. e
25. a & c (Score one point for each correct).
26. c
27. 1 c; 2 e; 3 b; 4 a; 5 d (Score 1 point if all are correct; 1/2 point if 3 are correct).
28. 1 c; 2 e; 3 d; 4 a; 5 b (Score 1 point if all are correct; 1/2 point if 3 are correct).
29. e
30. b
31. d
32. 1 c; 2 d; 3 e; 4 a; 5 b (Score 1 point if all are correct; 1/2 point if 3 are correct).